The Wildlife 123

Books from OWL
are published in Canada by
Greey de Pencier Books,
56 The Esplanade,
Suite 306,
Toronto, Ontario
M5E 1A7.

*The OWL colophon is
a trademark of the
Young Naturalist Foundation.
Greey de Pencier Books
is a licensed user
of trademarks of the
Young Naturalist Foundation.

This book was published
with the generous support
of the Canada Council
and the
Ontario Arts Council.

Text and illustrations © 1989
Jan Thornhill

Canadian Cataloguing in Publication Data

Thornhill, Jan
The wildlife 123

ISBN 0-920775-39-X

1. Animals – Juvenile literature. 2. Counting –
Juvenile literature. I. Title.

QL49.T56 1989   j591   C89-093356-1

Designed by Wycliffe Smith

Printed in Singapore

The Wildlife 123

A Nature Counting Book

Jan Thornhill

Greey de Pencier Books

1

One Panda

2

Two Giraffes

3

Three Starfish

4

Four Parrots

5
Five Tigers

6

Six Crocodiles

7

Seven Monkeys

8

Eight Camels

9

Nine Sparrows

10

Ten Mountain Goats

11

Eleven Elephants

12

Twelve Ants

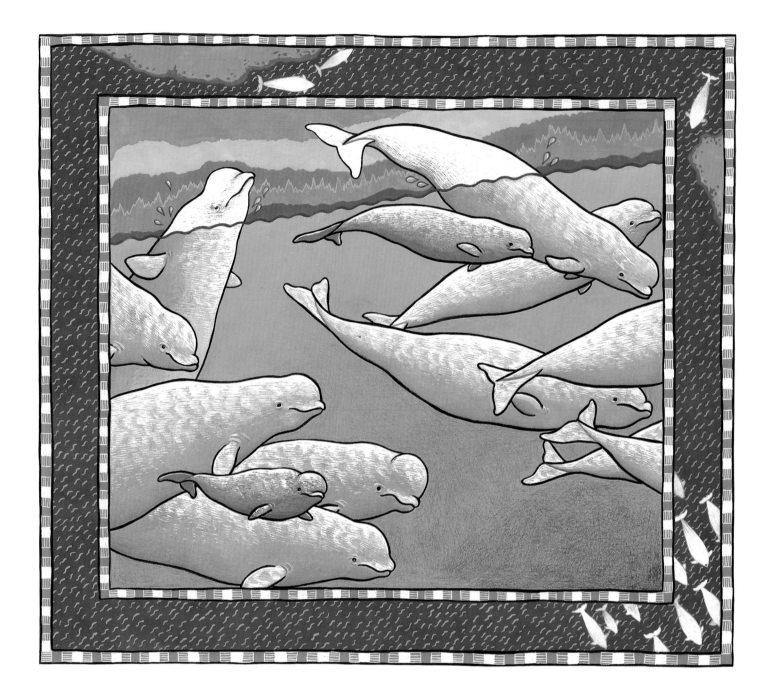

13

Thirteen Whales

14

Fourteen Lemurs

15

Fifteen Kangaroos

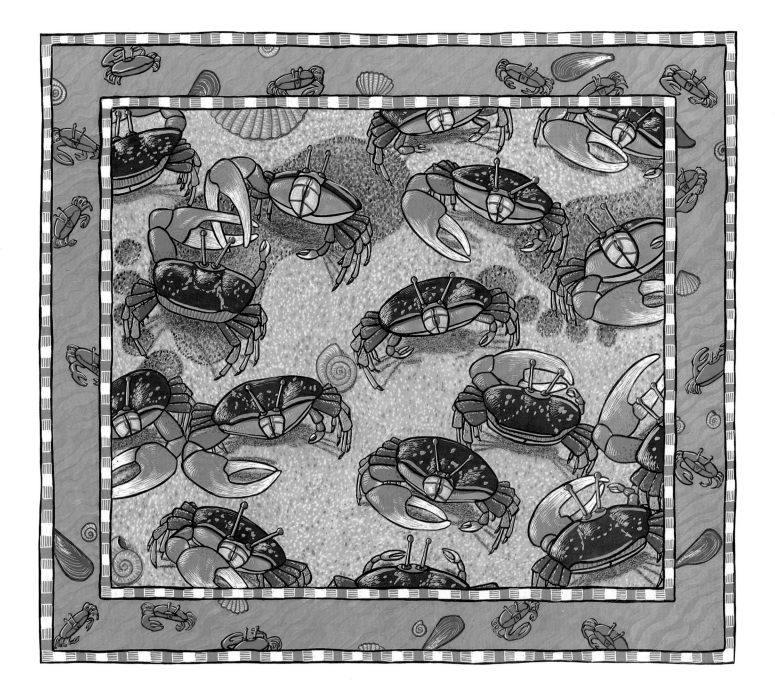

16

Sixteen Crabs

17

Seventeen Tortoises

18

Eighteen Prairie Dogs

19

Nineteen Walruses

20

Twenty Tropical Fish

25

Twenty-five Butterflies

50

Fifty Flamingos

100

One Hundred Penguins

1000

One Thousand Tadpoles

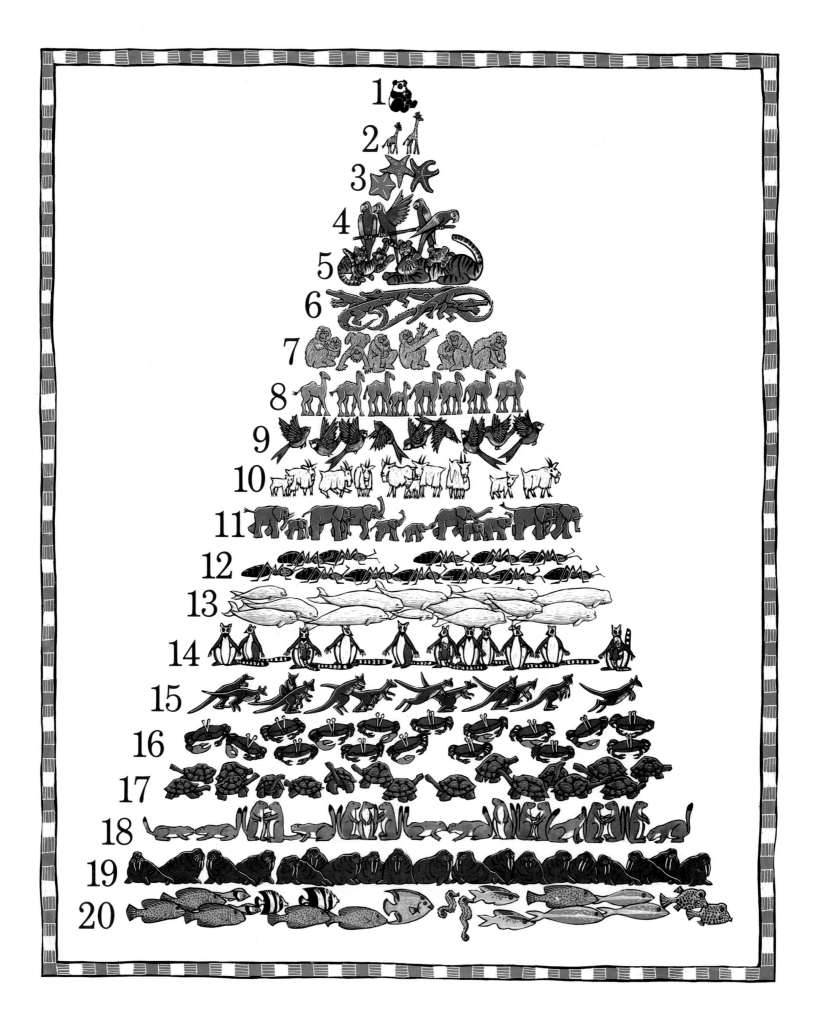

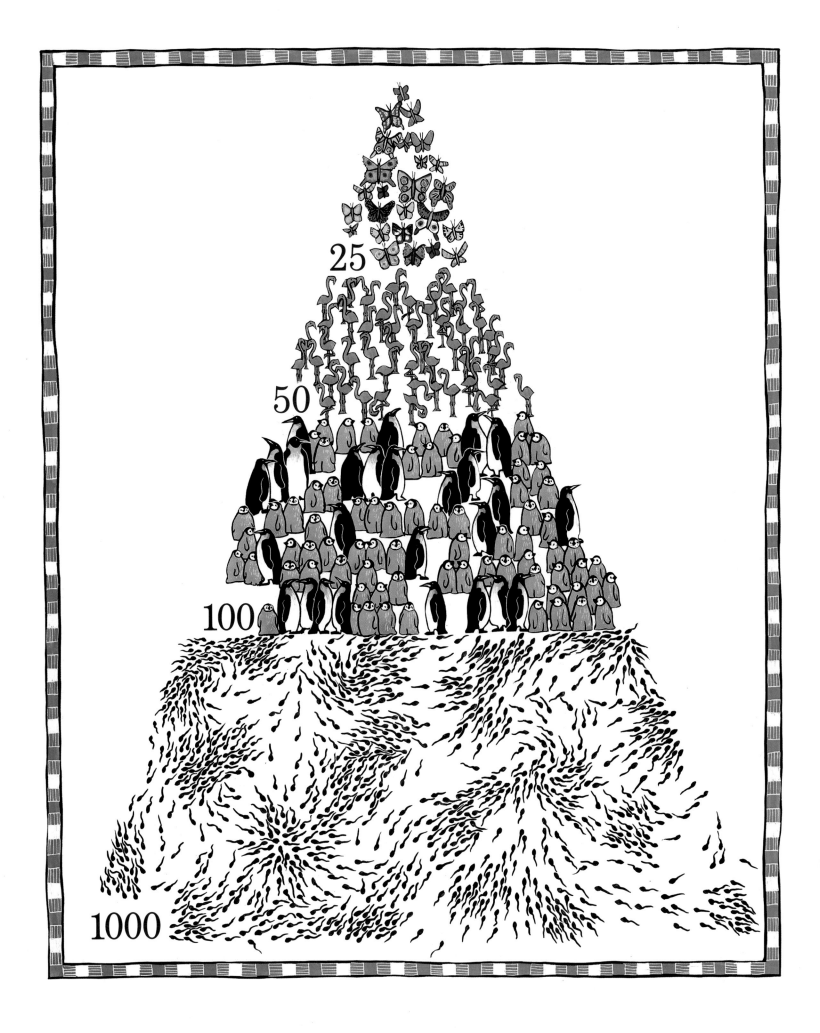

25

50

100

1000

Nature Notes

1
One Panda
in a bamboo forest

The Giant Panda, one of the world's rarest animals, is a native of China. Although bearlike, the panda may be related to the raccoon. It lives in high, mist-shrouded forests where bamboo, its favorite food, grows. A giant panda must eat huge quantities of bamboo every day to survive, and has even developed an extra "thumb" on its forepaws to help it grasp the stems. A newborn panda, pink and barely as large as a hamster, is carried in its mother's arms constantly for its first few weeks. The panda cub stays with its mother, growing and learning, until it is a year and a half old.

2
Two Giraffes
on the African savannah

The Giraffe stands three times the height of a man, and is the tallest creature on Earth. Tough hairs on its lips and a rubbery saliva coating its long, agile tongue make it possible for the giraffe to strip off and eat not only the leaves of such trees as the acacia, but also the twigs, branches and thorns. Because its head is held so high, the giraffe can see much further than zebras, wildebeests, ostriches and baboons, who depend on this graceful animal for danger signals when predators such as lions approach.

3
Three Starfish
in a tide pool

The Starfish or Seastar, found in oceans around the world, belongs to a spiny-skinned family of animals called the echinoderms. A starfish can have five, ten, even fifty arms (always in multiples of five) which are symmetrically arranged around the central disk where its mouth is found. Each arm has two rows of tube feet which the starfish uses to breathe, move and gather food. Although it has neither head nor brain, a starfish possesses the amazing power of regeneration: a single arm with only a bit of the central disk can grow into a complete animal within a year.

4
Four Parrots
in a rainforest

The Scarlet Macaw, found in South American rainforests, is one of the largest parrots in the world. The macaw has two toes pointing frontwards and two backwards, an arrangement ideally suited to clambering in trees and grasping the fruit and seeds that make up its diet. It is an extremely noisy bird, raucously yelping and screeching, especially in flight. The macaw, like other parrots, is an excellent mimic, and can imitate a wide range of sounds. Most macaws mate for life and nest in holes high in trees.

5
Five Tigers
in an Indian jungle

The dominant wildcat in Southeast Asia, the Tiger, makes its home in a variety of habitats ranging from mountain forests to lowland thickets. Tiger cubs are born blind and helpless. For two years they stay close to their mother, learning from her, and through rough-and-tumble play, the skills they will need to hunt and survive on their own. Because of hunting and the destruction of its habitat by man, the tiger population has declined sharply in this century. Recent establishment of reserves and protective status for this majestic cat has already helped its numbers increase.

6
Six Crocodiles
on the banks of the Nile

When a female Nile Crocodile is about ten years old, she lays her first clutch of eggs, burying them deep in sand beside water. When she hears croaking sounds, after nearly three months of guarding the nest, she digs up the eggs. The mother may help some of the tiny crocodiles hatch by gently rolling the eggs in her mouth to crack the shells. As they grow, crocodiles feed on larger and larger prey, quickly moving from insects to fish, rodents and birds. Competition with man for its habitat and food has made the Nile crocodile an endangered species.

7
Seven Monkeys
in the mountains of Japan

Snow Monkeys, a rare type of Japanese macaque, live in the mountains of Japan. Some of these monkeys live further north than any other primate except man. To protect themselves during the long, cold winters, snow monkeys grow fluffy coats and huddle together for warmth. One group has even discovered that they can warm themselves by bathing in the local hot springs. When other food is scarce, snow monkeys survive on the inner bark of trees no other monkey would consider food.

8
Eight Camels
in the Sahara desert

The one-humped Arabian Camel is closely related to the two-humped Bactrian camel of Asia and to the llamas and alpacas of South America. Supremely adapted for desert life, the camel has a short, wooly coat to insulate against the sun's heat, long eyelashes and nostril flaps to keep out blowing sand, broad, padded feet to make walking on sand easier, and the ability to go for several months without drinking water. Its height even assures that its head is held just above the level of swirling sand during desert storms. The camel's hump is not used for water storage but holds fat, acting as a reserve source of energy when food is unavailable.

9
Nine Sparrows
outside a kitchen window

The familiar, cocky House Sparrow, native to Eurasia and North Africa, now inhabits cities, towns and farmland all over the world. All house sparrows in North America are descendants of a small number released in New York City in 1850. They quickly spread, eating insects and seeds and sometimes damaging crops as they competed with native species for food. The house sparrow usually has three broods of young a year, and nests almost anywhere – in gutters and ventilation holes, on streetlamps and signs, and sometimes in trees.

10
Ten Mountain Goats
on the slopes of the Rockies

Despite its name and appearance, the Rocky Mountain Goat is really a mountain antelope. It inhabits craggy, remote slopes of the Rockies, far above the haunts of most of its natural enemies such as wolves, grizzly bears and cougars. It is surefooted and moves deliberately, easily climbing cliffs, balancing on narrow ledges, and jumping as much as 3m (10') from one rock to another. A mountain goat kid is playful but doesn't venture far from its mother. It seeks shelter under her during bad weather or when danger, such as a passing golden eagle, threatens.

11

Eleven Elephants
on the African plains

The African Elephant is the largest land animal on Earth. Its huge ears are much larger than those of its cousin, the Asiatic elephant. An elongated upper lip and nose combine to form its trunk, which is so sensitive it can pick up a single blade of grass. With its trunk, the elephant can also suck water up to squirt into its mouth or shower over its head and back. When a female elephant is ready to give birth, the other cows gather around to help. The calf is born covered with hair which it loses as it grows.

12

Twelve Ants
on a sidewalk

The Ant, a usually wingless insect, is found around the world. An ant colony is begun by a single queen who lays a small number of eggs. When the eggs hatch, the queen feeds the larvae until they reach maturity. These adult workers are all female. They take over the business of the colony, digging tunnels and store-rooms, tending eggs, feeding larvae, searching for food and protecting the nest, leaving the queen free for a life of laying eggs. After a few years the colony may contain hundreds of ants. At this time the queen produces a winged group of males and queens. These ants fly from the nest and the young queens establish new colonies.

13

Thirteen Whales
in Arctic waters

The Beluga or White Whale is sometimes called the sea canary because of its "singing". Through air passages in its rounded forehead or melon, it produces a wide variety of whistles, ticks, bell-like tones, squeals, chirps and sounds similar to those made by children playing in the distance. The beluga, a predominantly Arctic animal, is a small whale rarely exceeding 4.5m (15') in length.

The bluish- or brownish-gray calves become lighter as they age, turning completely white by the time they are five or six years old. Belugas feed in small herds on marine animals such as shrimp, fish, squid and snails.

14

Fourteen Lemurs
on a Madagascar forest floor

Ring-tailed Lemurs, related to monkeys and apes, are native only to Madagascar, an island off the southeast coast of Africa. The ring-tail lives in troops of five to twenty animals headed by one or more older females who defend their territory against intruders. They are active during the day, sunbathing, grooming one another, wandering about with their tails in the air and leaping from tree to tree eating fruit, seeds, leaves and bark. A newborn ring-tail is carried in its mother's arms for a month before it is strong enough to cling to her back as she moves about. Ring-tails and other lemurs are threatened by the destruction of their rainforest home.

15

Fifteen Kangaroos
in the Australian outback

The Red Kangaroo, found only in Australia, is a marsupial, an animal with a pouch for carrying its offspring. A newborn kangaroo, the size of a bean, "swims" arm over arm through its mother's fur until it reaches her pouch where it nurses for six months. The joey first leaves the pouch when it is seven and a half months old, but it returns frequently, tumbling in headfirst at any sign of danger, until it is too large to fit. The red kangaroo is an excellent two-footed jumper and, using its tail for balance, can leap 10m (33').

16

Sixteen Crabs
on a sandy beach

The diminutive, sideways-walking Fiddler Crab lives on sandy and muddy shores around the world.

One of the male's two claws is much larger than the other. He uses this claw to signal or for ritual combat when protecting his tiny territory. Each crab digs a hole to hide in when the tide comes in, plugging it with mud so that there is just enough air to breathe until the tide goes out again.

17

Seventeen Tortoises
on the Galapagos Islands

The Giant Tortoise of the Galapagos Islands can weigh as much as 275kg (600lb) and is probably a descendant of South American tortoises that floated on logs or debris to the islands thousands of years ago.
Because it is a cold-blooded reptile, the Galapagos tortoise settles down to sleep in shallow, tepid rainwater pools to keep warm during the night. Instead of teeth, it has sharp-edged jaws for nipping off the grasses, berries and cacti that make up its diet.

18

Eighteen Prairie Dogs
on the North American plains

Prairie Dogs live in towns composed of many coteries or small family groups, each with its own observation mounds and network of underground tunnels, listening posts, store-rooms, rooms for eliminating waste, and nest chambers. Using different barks, this rodent defends its territory, warns against danger such as the approach of a coyote, or gives the all-clear signal when it is safe for others to come out again. In the late spring, young prairie dogs leave their grass-lined nests to explore the world above ground where they eat grasses, roots and seeds, and take part in social activities such as kissing, grooming, playing, wrestling and basking in the sun.

19

Nineteen Walruses
on an Arctic ice floe

The Walrus, an Arctic mammal closely related to sea lions and seals, lives and travels in large herds.

This huge animal, weighing an average of one ton, is protected from the cold by a layer of oily blubber up to 15cm (6") thick. The walrus uses its ivory tusks, which are overgrown canine teeth, for jousting or for hoisting its massive bulk up onto ice floes. It finds mussels in the dark depths of the icy waters with its thick mustache of long, stiff whiskers, and feeds for up to two days at a time before lounging for another two days on land. A mother walrus teaches her single offspring to swim by carrying it piggyback or holding it between her fore-flippers as she swims.

20

Twenty Tropical Fish
on a coral reef

A dazzling variety of fish are found on coral reefs, which are made up of the stony skeletons of billions of coral polyps. Most reef fish are territorial, and defend their food, hiding places, egg-laying areas and night-resting spots. Reef fish are found in a myriad of shapes, sizes and colors; some eat algae while others are predators or scavengers. Pictured counter-clockwise from the top left are: yellow snapper, a queen angel fish, blue-head wrasse, banded butterfly fish, a spotted trunk fish, damsel fish, a queen triggerfish, a trumpet fish and a sea horse. Twenty redhinds are shown in the border.

25

Twenty-five Butterflies
resting in a tree

The North American Monarch Butterfly can be seen congregating in large numbers in the fall. Incredibly, these delicate-winged insects migrate several thousand kilometres south to their wintering grounds, some as far as Mexico. There they hibernate in the same large groups before returning north in the spring to lay their eggs.
The eggs hatch into tiny caterpillars with huge appetites. The caterpillars eat and grow until they are large enough to pupate. When the adult butterfly finally emerges from its chrysalis, it has enough fat stored in its body to give it energy for the long flight south.

50

Fifty Flamingos
in shallow waters

Huge flocks of pink Flamingos are found in a wide range of tropical and warm temperate areas around the world. These flocks, sometimes numbering a million or more, spend most of their lives wading in shallow alkaline lakes. They hold their curiously-shaped bills upside down in the water to filter out algae and small marine animals for food. Because the areas surrounding salt and soda lakes are often barren, flamingos have few predators. Females lay a single egg in a mud-mound nest, protected from flooding and heat. Both parents produce milk which they feed to their fluffy gray young.

100

One Hundred Penguins
in the Antarctic

The Emperor Penguin is flightless, and stands an amazing 1.2m (4') tall. Although clumsy on land, it is the most expert of all swimming birds, as agile while chasing squid underwater as a fish. The emperor lives in rookeries of up to a million birds and lays its single egg in the dark, cold Antarctic winter. For two months the male holds the egg on top of his feet, keeping it warm with a fold of skin on his belly. He does not eat during this time. When the chicks hatch, the females return to relieve the males and feed the chicks their first meal.

1000

One Thousand Tadpoles
in a pond

In the spring, frogs and toads lay hundreds of jelly-protected eggs in ponds. Each egg hatches into a larva or tiny Tadpole which soon develops gills for breathing as well as eyes, a mouth and a tail. Feeding on waterweeds, the growing tadpole gradually develops legs and lungs. Eventually the tail is absorbed into the body to provide food for the final metamorphosis of the tadpole into an adult amphibian, and the young frog or toad swims to land.

The Wildlife 123

1	9	17
One Panda	Nine Sparrows	Seventeen Tortoises
2	10	18
Two Giraffes	Ten Mountain Goats	Eighteen Prairie Dogs
3	11	19
Three Starfish	Eleven Elephants	Nineteen Walruses
4	12	20
Four Parrots	Twelve Ants	Twenty Tropical Fish
5	13	25
Five Tigers	Thirteen Whales	Twenty-five Butterflies
6	14	50
Six Crocodiles	Fourteen Lemurs	Fifty Flamingos
7	15	100
Seven Monkeys	Fifteen Kangaroos	One Hundred Penguins
8	16	1000
Eight Camels	Sixteen Crabs	One Thousand Tadpoles